Memories Of Scottish Scenes And Sabbaths More Than Eighty Years Ago

Alexander Kennedy

In the interest of creating a more extensive selection of rare historical book reprints, we have chosen to reproduce this title even though it may possibly have occasional imperfections such as missing and blurred pages, missing text, poor pictures, markings, dark backgrounds and other reproduction issues beyond our control. Because this work is culturally important, we have made it available as a part of our commitment to protecting, preserving and promoting the world's literature. Thank you for your understanding.

Memories of Scottish Scenes and Sabbaths more than Eighty years ago;

OR,

SKETCHES OF RELIGIOUS LIFE AMONG THE PEASANTRY OF AYRSHIRE EARLY IN THE NINETEENTH CENTURY.

BY THE LATE

REV. ALEXANDER KENNEDY,

DUNBARTON, ONTARIO.

WITH PREFACE BY THE

REV. J. K. SCOTT, B.D.,

FRASERBURGH.

EDINBURGH:

ANDREW ELLIOT, 17 PRINCES STREET.

1902.

CONTENTS.

———✦———

PREFACE.

THE following pages are a reprint of some articles that appeared in the *Canadian United Presbyterian Magazine* in 1860 and 1861. The writer's name was not given, but they are known to be from the pen of the late Rev. Alexander Kennedy of Dunbarton, Pickering, Canada West, as the Province was at that time called. Mr Kennedy when young had seen and taken part in what he describes. He was born in the parish of New Cumnock, Ayrshire, and brought up on the farm of Dalricket Mill, of which his father was tenant. The eldest son of a family of thirteen, he attended with the others the Secession Church of Old Cumnock, in which congregation his father was an elder. Having studied for the ministry of the Secession Church, he was sent out in 1835 by Greyfriars Congregation, Glasgow, as a missionary to Trinidad, where he laboured for about fourteen years, preaching to both the Europeans and the Negroes. He took a very prominent part in protesting against and opposing the cruel wrongs which the negroes at that time were suffering in the island. In 1849, his health having completely broken down, he left Trinidad and went to Canada, with little hope of ever being able to do more than preach the Gospel for a short time to a few of the straggling settlers in some remote locality where the regular means of grace did not exist.

But the change of scene and the more bracing climate of Canada soon restored him to health and vigour. Before long three different congregations called him to be their pastor. One of these calls he accepted, and for full forty years he was an active and highly esteemed minister of the Canadian Church. He died at Welland, Ontario, in 1892, in his eighty-ninth year, having demitted his charge some years previously.

A venerable elder, Mr David Scott of Boghead, Girvan, having a set of the Magazines containing the articles, thought that the vivid glimpses there given of how our fathers worshipped God in the sanctuary and in the home were worthy of preservation, and might with profit be read by some in our day. He proposed, therefore, to have them reprinted, and asked the present writer to prepare a few explanatory notes. So the articles are here reproduced, mainly for the sake of those, and they are many, who are related to Mr Kennedy, or have some knowledge of him, and of the congregation and district of which he wrote. If the articles should interest others into whose hands they may come, the gratification of the venerable friend, now in his ninety-first year, at whose instance they are reprinted, will be all the greater.

In whatever respects the present generation may be in advance of our fathers who lived when the last century was in its teens, in at least two very important matters we seem to be behind them. These are: —(1) Regard for and improvement of the Christian Sabbath ; (2) The religious instruction of the young in their own home by their own parents.

The secularising of the Sabbath which has been carried to such an extent in this country, and the apparently widespread neglect by parents of the religious training of their children, are cause for concern and anxiety. They work to lower the moral tone, and weaken the moral strength, not only of the church, but of the nation. For no nation can be, either in the highest sense or enduringly, prosperous and strong, except in so far as the people know and practise righteousness, and this can be attained only in the measure in which they fear God and keep His commandments.

In cultivating and producing these moral fruits of righteousness, the schoolmaster can never take the place nor do the work of the parent.

The picture drawn by Mr Kennedy of the religious instruction given in the home of his youth, is true, it is believed, of many other homes at that time. It describes what was then the common practice in the Christian homes of Scotland, and it would be well for the churches and for the nation if there were a general return to such parental training.

When the articles first appeared, names of both persons and places were omitted. The reasons for such omissions have, it is believed, passed away, and so the names have been supplied so far as known. Foot-notes have been added where these seemed necessary. In the title the word *forty* has been changed to *eighty*.

FRASERBURGH,
  August 1902.

Memories of Scottish Scenes and Sabbaths
more than Eighty years ago.

——•◦•——

I.

THE SECESSION CHURCH AT CUMNOCK.

IN the home of my youth the Sabbath day was
wholly reserved for religious exercises, except so far
as works of necessity and mercy claimed attention.
On other mornings the household were up betimes
and busily engaged in the varied employments of the
farm, in the house and out of doors. On the Sabbath
the inmates did not rise quite so early, but were up in
good time to attend to the needs of man and beast,
and prepare for going to church, which was about
five miles distant. It was necessary that some should
remain at home to look after the house and the cattle,
but those who could be spared got "ready for the Kirk,"
and set out, the young and vigorous mostly on foot,
while "the guidman" and "the guidwife," with perhaps an aged neighbour and some of the younger

children, would ride in a cart. A gig was at that time
a rarity among the farmers of the district. When "the
guidwife" was detained at home, "the guidman"
would sometimes, instead of taking a cart, ride to
church on his hardy little Highland pony "Donald,"
a beast that was as docile as a lamb when his master
was on his back, but by no means so gentle when
some other was in charge, as some occasionally found
to their cost. "The lang man on the wee powny"
was a somewhat conspicuous figure on the road, and
attracted notice and remark. On the first part of the
journey only a few others were to be seen on the bare
and exposed highway, but gradually the number increased as each farmhouse and cottage sent forth its
quota, until as the end of the journey approached the
road was thickly dotted with individuals and little
groups all going the same way.

The little town of Cumnock is reached, and great
numbers are pouring in from all directions to engage
in the public solemnities of the Sabbath, in their
respective places of worship At that time there were
only two churches in the town, viz., the Parish Church
and the Meeting House, as the latter was called.
Now there are, I believe, at least five churches—the
effect of sectarianism rather than of increased popula-
tion. The congregation assembling in the plain un-
pretentious Meeting House was far larger, and more
influential, in every desirable sense, than that which
met in the capacious and dingy Kirk. The blight of
Moderatism lay on many a parish kirk in that part of

the country in those days, and that of Cumnock was
one of the many. Its pulpit was then, and had been
for a long time previously, occupied by Dr Miller, a
moral, amiable, but feeble-minded man, though learned
withal, as report had it. But his theological tenets
were said to have a tinge of Socinianism—to man the
most dreary, and to God the most dishonouring, of all
Christian creeds. Whether he was justly chargeable
with such fatal heterodoxy I cannot affirm. Certain
it is he was no great preacher, and piety was by no
means rife among his people. However, he was not
wanting in tenderness. At times he was melted to
tears while delivering his sermons, which was infer-
entially accounted for as follows by the Laird of
Logan (one of his parishioners), whose witticisms and
waggeries have long had a national notoriety. Some
simple countryman, unskilled in tracing effect to its
cause, asked the laird why it was that "the Doctor
aye grat when he preach't." "Hoot man," said the
laird, "put you into the pu'pit, and gie ye as little to
say, and ye wud greet too."

The parish was rather populous, and the Doctor's
Kirk had a goodly number of retainers, as Established
Churches will generally have, irrespective of the
character of their creeds, as it is of no little importance
with mere professors and careless Christians to have
their creed sanctioned and their worship supported by
the Government. However, despite the temptation of
seemingly gratis ordinances under the sunshine of
political power, and the favouritism of the Marquis of

Bute and the parochial squirearchy, the Meeting
House, as already stated, had by far the larger number
of adherents and weekly worshippers. The membership amounted to about 700, gathered out of nine or
ten parishes; I think I have heard it stated that, in
the earlier days of the Secession, there were members
of this Church to be found in thirteen or fourteen
parishes.

In my day it was no uncommon thing for members
and adherents to travel from ten to fourteen miles to
worship in that house of God. Surely there was some
good thing, in their hearts, towards the Lord God,
drawing them so far, and that without grudge, to the
place where He had recorded His name. Memory
readily suggests two families—worthy families verily
—respectively distant from the Church about eight
miles and nine miles,—the one consisting of two elderly
females, and the other of three brothers and the wife
of one of them, all past life's noon, who were remark-
ably regular in their attendance, though the distance
was invariably travelled a-foot,—in the one case from
necessity and in the other from choice. That Sabbath
must have been tempestuous indeed, or the roads all
but unpassable, that witnessed their seats vacant in
the sanctuary. Doubtless they felt the force of the
Apostolic injunction, " Forsake not the assembling of
yourselves together," and proved in their sweet experience that it is no vain thing to serve the Lord.
Their estimate of public ordinances must have been
akin to that of David, when he deliberately avowed

that a day spent in the courts of the Lord's house " is better than a thousand."

In those days, and in those parts, religious individuals and families never dreamed of absenting themselves from ordinances because of ordinarily inclement weather. Out of a period bordering on twenty years, I can only recall with anything like certitude, two Sabbaths on which the family to which I had the privilege to belong were all shut up at home by the weather. The detention in one case was caused by one of those unusually heavy snowfalls and dreadful drifts, when the snow-wreath becomes the winding sheet of many a shepherd who tends his flock on the dreary moors and in the rugged glens to be found amid the mountain scenery of Scotia. I have never witnessed a snowstorm in Canada that equalled in blinding bitterness what I have often seen and felt in the land of my birth.

The Meeting House to which the greater number of church-goers wended their way, was a large, unadorned, but substantial building, erected early in the last quarter of the last century. Yes, the figures 1777, painted on the partition behind the pulpit, staring in the face the entrants at the front door, start up and distinctly stand out before my mind's eye at the present moment. Fully fifty years have passed, since, led by the hand of a parent or under the care of an elder sister, I entered that door of that house of God and gazed in wonderment at these numerical symbols —ignorant then of their powers and of their deep and sacred meaning, as indicating the date when the world's Saviour was born, as well as telling the time when the house was erected for His worship.

Connected with the building of the Meeting House some noteworthy providential incidents occurred, which I well remember hearing related by one of the fathers of the church. The Secession was looked on with anything but favour by the aristocracy. The contempt cherished and the opposition manifested were stronger and more general far than toward that auspicious modern Secession which issued in the Free Church in Scotland. During the days of the Erskines, and for long years after, Secession principles had a hard fight for existence in many parts of the country, and their stalwart maintainers were subjected to much trouble and no trifling sacrifices. Those residing in and around the town of Cumnock had every available obstacle put in their way to prevent them from erecting a place of worship. Such was the enmity and inimical influence of Lord Dumfries, that for a time a site for a church could not be obtained. Neither he, nor any one else possessed of any land, would sell a portion for such a purpose. Intelligence of this fact got abroad, and a female residing in a neighbouring parish, and, if I mistake not, herself attached to the Established Church, had compassion on the conscientious and ill-treated Seceders, and either gifted or sold (I am not certain which) a small piece of ground owned by her at the "toun fit," and just as near out of it as possible. However, it was a suitable and lovely spot, just between and at the junction of two streams, viz., the Glaisnock and the classic Lugar that flows "behind yon hills."

Having thus obtained ground on which to erect their church, another serious difficulty presented itself. With what were they to build it? The same enmity and influence that had kept them for a while from obtaining land, now prevented them getting building materials at anything like convenient distance. The quarries in the neighbourhood were all closed to them. The stones had to be brought from the next parish, and I presume the lime also. As much sand was got when digging the foundation as served to make mortar till the walls rose a little, perhaps a foot or two, above the level of the ground; a further supply of sand was not to be had, though in the channel of the river or stream close by, not many yards distant, a sand-bed, bared by the summer's drought, lay as if laughing and mocking at the wants of the builders. But though quite at hand and tempting to their shovels as it must have been, yet it was legally beyond their reach. My Lord Dumfries claimed the channel of the stream and all its contents. Of course the masons had to cease operations for want of sand to manufacture mortar.

Thus the work stood for a time, but whether for a few days only or for weeks I cannot tell. However, in no great time Providence supplied them with abundance of sand without putting them to any trouble or cost, not even the cost of cartage, and by means as little expected by the friends as by the foes of dissent. The Lord sent "a plenteous rain," causing an unusually high flood—in all likelihood a "Lammas flood." The two streams which here united overflowed their banks, covering the low walls of the arrested building. When the waters subsided it was found that a large quantity of sand brought down by the rushing stream had been deposited within and around the walls—amply sufficient, it was said, to complete the building. In this there was no miracle, but what Christian can doubt, or refuse, adoringly and gratefully to acknowledge, that the Lord in this case commissioned his ever obedient servants the elements to do a timely service to His struggling people?

I have to beg of the reader to pardon my "havering" digressions. On commencing this article I intended to proceed forthwith to record some memories of the Sabbath services in the Meeting House at Cumnock when I was a lad, but have somehow wandered wide of my purpose. Let me now speak of these services and of him who conducted them, the Rev. Mr Wilson,* a man remembered by many, and worthy of remembrance, for he was "a workman that needed not to be ashamed." He invariably commenced the Sabbath services by reading and *prefacing* a portion of a psalm. This part of the service occupied from twenty minutes

---

* The Rev. David Wilson, Minister at Old Cumnock, 1788-1822. A short life of this remarkable man by the late Rev. P. Mearns, Coldstream, was pubished in 1858 under the title of "The Devoted Minister."

to half an hour; and an interesting and profitable exercise it was. Pity the practice has fallen into general desuetude. But few ministers could preface as Mr Wilson did. He had a strong practical mind, and an earnest and fervid mode of address. His remarks on the psalm secured the attention and solemnised the minds of the audience, and were a fine preparative for singing it with the understanding and the heart. And the singing was usually of a very cordial character, though perhaps not distinguished for the sweetness of its melody.

The sinful, God-contemning fashion did not then and there prevail, of sitting mute in God's house while his praises were being sung. It is very sad to witness persons in a worshipping assembly not only sitting mute while the service of praise is proceeding, but carefully closing and constricting their lips as if afraid they might be even suspected of praising a redeeming God. God was not praised by proxy in the Meeting House at Cumnock. There was no choir "to do the singing" exclusively, as in some churches on this Continent and elsewhere. It seemed as if the heavenly service of praise was felt to be an individual duty and privilege, as it undoubtedly is. I have something further to tell about the singing, and how, and with what difficulty, it was revolutionized, but these and my narrative of the remaining Sabbath services must wait a future opportunity.

II.

SECESSION SINGING.

IN my early youth, the psalmody in the Meeting House at Cumnock was of the olden type — of Covenanter character. Every line, before being sung, was read aloud with musical monotony by the precentor. And repeating tunes, if known at all in the district, were conscientiously abjured in the songs of the sanctuary. Their introduction, in after years, was fruitful of dispeace and ill-feeling,—a cause of grief to many a godly heart. The tunes generally sung were solemn and time-hallowed,—tunes that erst and often had been heard in heaven, from the moors and mountain-fastnesses of Scotland :—

> . . . . In those "days of darkness and blood,
> When the minister's hame was the mountain and wud."
> . . . . "When the standard of Zion,
> All bloody and torn, 'mang the heather was lyin'."

We can well forgive (we should perhaps say admire) the partiality for the music of the martyrs, cherished by the pious of a past generation. Its richness is more than compensation for its asserted rudeness; and the fact that it had, times untold, conveyed up into Jehovah's eager ear, the desires, the hopes and

the fears, the confidence and thanksgivings, of His
persecuted people, might well impart to it sweetness,
and invest it with a sacred character, in the estimation
of our forefathers, to whom tradition told—with far
more emphasis than history does to us—the bloody
tragedies enacted by the recreant and remorseless
rulers of their native land. Could we sing "with the
understanding and the heart," as the martyrs sang,—
with a faith as strong, an affection as pure and ardent,
and a hope as bright, we would desire no other
collocation of musical sounds than that employed
by them.

Musical taste, even with the pious, changed with
the times. We marked, with some interest, a measure
of that change, and still remember some incidents, of
a local character, connected therewith, which, to our
then somewhat volatile and untutored mind, bordered
close on the ludicrous. Example, like water, runs
down hill ; and as more rapid and repeating tunes, as
well as singing without reading the line, began to
obtain in the more aristocratic churches in the
metropolis and larger cities of the land, it was no long
time ere the younger members of village and land-
ward churches felt anxious to have the same practices
adopted in their respective Sabbath assemblies.

But serious difficulties lay in the way. As was to
be expected, these innovations were sternly opposed
by the aged, who were devoutly wedded to the olden
ways of worship. And at that time there were many
in the congregation of Cumnock whose grey hairs

and godliness gave them deserved influence. The precentor did not dare to sing any new-fangled tunes, or to dispense with the reading of the line.

But a junior and forward Elder, gifted with musical talent and a large amount of confidence, took the desk on one occasion, and started, I suppose, some new tune, and proceeded to sing it without reading the line, to the consternation, and devout indignation doubtless, of not a few in the assembly. On reaching the close of the first verse, the minister, Mr Wilson, rose hurriedly, and in a very excited manner, touched the head of the daring innovator, the usual mode of indicating from the pulpit that the psalmody should cease. Instead of remaining silent, as desired, the erring Elder, wishing to mend matters by instantly returning to use and wont, began to read out the next line. This was more than the patience of the worthy minister could bear, who, quick as thought, reached out his arm over the shoulder of the presumptuous and persistent singer, and rather roughly, by rapid and repeated movements or strokes of the hand, attempted to close the psalm-book, a proceeding that gave occasion to some of the rather light-minded and waggish to say that "the Minister cuffed the Elder's lugs." The scene was exciting but short, terminating prematurely and abruptly the singing of the closing or after-sermon psalm, leaving the excellent but somewhat irritable minister in no desirable mood of mind for offering up the parting prayer. The whole is yet fresh in my memory.

It would be a good while, no doubt—but how long
I cannot tell—ere any further attempt was made to
interfere with the good old way of singing, by
omitting to read the line, or by introducing out-
landish five-lined tunes. However, the wish for these
changes not only remained but waxed,—for music,
vocal and instrumental, was cultivated assiduously,
and with no mean measure of success, by numbers of
the young residing in the town and connected with
the congregation.

By and bye another and a more successful effort
was made to bring the singing in the Meeting House
up to the fashion of the day. Who the officiating
minister was on that rather memorable occasion, I
do not now remember. Probably advantage was
taken of the presence of a stranger minister. However, one day the precentor sang on without reading
the line, and in all likelihood gave the last line of
every stanza a second singing. This, in the estimation of some, was outrageous and utterly intolerable,
demanding on their part instant and emphatic protest.
Two of the aggrieved had the fortitude to protest by
an act far more expressive of disapprobation and
disgust than any words they could have uttered or
written. They sprang to their feet, left their pews,
and made for the door, and their tread down the aisle
or pass was neither that of sylphs nor such as suits a
sickroom. Everybody knows that a person's gait
goes far to unfold the master-feeling of his heart, and
that his tramp unmistakably indicates the amount of

passion moving him for the moment, which, in some instances, can claim principle as its prompter, if not its parent.

It would be uncharitable and very wrong to place the act of those two persons wholly to the account of prejudice, pride, and passion. I verily believe they were prompted primarily, and to a large extent, by zeal for God's house and worship; but whether that zeal was according to knowledge, is another question. I believe all who knew them would, without hesitation, give them a place among the excellent of the earth. Both of them outlived their original horror at the modern mode of psalmody. It is twenty-five years since one of them was called away, doubtless to join the choir in the upper sanctuary, where there are no innovations, no jarring notes heard, and no ruffled feelings known. The other, I hope, yet lives, and has for nearly forty years sung God's praises weekly in that same assembly, with both pleasure and profit, despite unread lines and repeating tunes.

The new mode of singing had now got a foothold in the Meeting House, and it kept it, and gradually gained ground. However, for a good while there were numerous, though comparatively silent and unobtrusive, protests against the supposed graceless practice. Some of the aged and more rigid quietly opened their bibles and read a passage of scripture while the psalm was being sung in the new style.

But there was one man—a truly godly man, and by no means deficient in shrewdness and knowledge

—whose opposition to these musical novelties was indomitable.* He sat, with several others, within the railing that surrounded the pulpit, that he might the better hear the preacher. Than he, no one sang the praises of God more cordially when the old mode was adhered to; but when the new mode was adopted, which for a good while was not more than once at each service, he invariably closed his book with a clash, took off his "specs," and sat mum, his features vigorously expressing more than disapprobation. Had a master painter caught him then,—transferring the spirit and language of his looks to canvas, it would have been an immortal work, and might have been labelled, "The Picture of Holy Indignation." On such occasions, after retiring from the church, and on his way home, a distance of about two miles, usually accompanied by a number of eager listeners, he was unsparing in his denunciations of the Popish and play-actor practices that had been introduced. One of his remarks was,—and the tone of sovereign contempt in which it was uttered yet lingers in my mind,—"If they had just an auld box organ yoner, they wud noo be complete."

This type of Scottish character, belonging to a past generation, was pestered not a little for his staunch conservatism of ancient religious forms. Some of the frolicsome youths, for the purpose of annoying, would rap at his window of nights, and call out,—"Cooper" (so named after his trade),

* Cooper Howat (?).

"Cooper, th're aye singin' yon way in the Meeting
House yet," a fact of which the good man needed
not to be apprized, but the announcement of which
not only interrupted his slumbers, but sadly inter-
fered with his inner equanimity.

But more than enough, for the ends of interest and
profit, has been said about the singing. It is high
time that the other services of the Sabbath engage
our attention.

The prefaced psalm being sung, solemn prayer
was offered up, and Mr Wilson's Sabbath morning
prayer was usually of rather remarkable character.
It was long, though by no means too long for the
really devout, but it had little or nothing of that
indefiniteness and generalization that often pertain
to pulpit prayers. There was a speciality and appro-
priateness in the petitions presented of a noteworthy
character. Sickness and death were almost weekly
at work in some corner of his numerous and widespread congregation, and his pleadings on behalf of
the sick, the dying and the bereaved were, as regarded
his hearers, singularly arrestive, and, it is to be hoped,
with God prevalent. The wrestling earnestness of the
man of God could not be unheeded, or soon forgotten.

There were but few Sabbaths in a year on which
the precentor, at the rising of the vast congregation
to the morning prayer, had not some name, or names,
to enunciate prefaced with the solemn words,
"Remember in prayer"—or followed by the equally
solemn and more saddening statement,—"apparently

dying," or "in great distress, requests the prayers of this congregation." Such announcements had a beneficial and hallowing influence on the assembly. They were at once prompters and aids to devotion. To be told, at the moment of approach to a throne of grace, that some neighbour or acquaintance was in the furnace of affliction, or in conflict with the last enemy, forcefully called forth common and Christly sympathy, which is a fine preparatory for prayer, and intensifies devotion.

We do think it were well if it were more the custom in Canada to solicit, after the old fashion, the prayers of congregations for the afflicted and dying of their number. The suppliants themselves would profit largely, and who dares to doubt that blessings manifold and precious would be vouchsafed to distressed and dying ones in answer to the believing prayers offered up by God's people assembled in His house, and again at their family altars and in their closets. Why should the members of Christ's body in Canada, united as they are by the electric chain of sanctified sympathy and love, have any delicacy or hesitancy, when trysted with trouble, in asking a special interest in the prayers of their fellow members? The guilt of neglect, if not a darker type of culpability, is chargeable, we fear, on many churches in regard to this matter. Afflicted ones there are, and will be, among God's people while dwellers on earth. Would then that we heard in our Sabbath assemblies the request, "remember in prayer"—that solemn toll to a sacred duty from the chamber of sickness and the bed of death.

It was the invariable practice of the minister of Cumnock to lecture on a portion of Scripture in the forenoon of Sabbath,—a profitable practice that still obtains, I believe, in favoured Scotland, and should undoubtedly be more common in Canada than it is. It is far better fitted than sermonising for communicating Scripture knowledge, and is more after the type of primitive preaching than the modern mode of discoursing. Mr Wilson did not wander through the Bible, selecting a passage here, and another there, as the subject of lecture, but took up one of its component books, and lectured through it in consecutive order, taking at each time a goodly number of verses.

I cannot speak minutely or with aught like desirable certitude of his lectures, as, to my sin and sorrow, I did not always listen to them with that attention and interest which I ought. I fear that I foolishly felt the lecture to be the heaviest portion of the Sabbath services. My impression is that his lectures were not burdened with verbal criticism or philological disquisition, and that a plain statement of the doctrines understood to be taught in the passage, and an earnest enforcement of the duties therein enjoined, were their sole characteristics. That they were eminently profitable there can be no doubt, for many in that congregation attained to an enviable degree of scriptural knowledge and heavenly grace under his ministrations.

Still I am inclined to think his *forte* lay not so much
in lecturing as in preaching, of which I shall briefly
speak, after telling how the interval between the
forenoon and afternoon service was spent; unless I
learn that the readers of my homely tale are tired.

III.

THE INTERVAL, AND HOW IT WAS SPENT.

DURING the winter months there was no intermission of the Sabbath services in the Meeting House at Cumnock, from their commencement at eleven o'clock a.m. till their close at two o'clock p.m., or perhaps a little later. This arrangement was necessary to allow the worshippers to get home, though not all of them, ere night set in. Many of them, as already stated, lived at a great distance from that house of God, in which they weekly worshipped. Indeed, so far had some of them to travel, that, in the dead of winter, darkness covered their path before they reached their habitations.

But during the summer months there was an interval, of at least an hour, between the forenoon and afternoon service. That hour was variously spent, though, generally, in no way unsuitable to the sacredness of the Sabbath, or unbecoming the Christian character. That hour witnessed the communion of saints—the interchange of friendly and affectionate greetings and inquiries, and sometimes also of pro-

fitable and sweet converse about "the one thing need-
ful;" about the hopes and fears, the joys and sorrows,
incident to the sojourn of heaven's heirs on earth.

It was a pleasant hour, and not wanting in virtual
worship, though of a coterie character. Having
emerged with soft and solemn tread from the
sanctuary, the great congregation occupied the open
space about the church, and for a few minutes there
were cordial shaking of hands, reciprocated smiles,
and more than neighbourly—ay, even warm-hearted
Christian interrogatives anent personal and family
welfare. The scene witnessed at mid-day dismissal
might have called forth the exclamation seldom
prompted, "Behold how these Christians love one
another!" By-and-bye the crowd began to melt
away, some retiring to the houses of their relatives or
friends in the town; others, in little bands, often of two
or three, slowly wended their way along the beautiful,
romantic, and copse-wooded banks of the Lugar, or
to the lanes and bye-ways leading into the neighbouring fields, there quietly to converse and meditate.
And, according to the testimony of my experience
and observation, the converse of these little parties
was seldom indeed of a purely worldly character. In
general it was less or more in unison with the sacredness of the day and the solemn services just closed,
and soon to be resumed.

There might be seen here and there, also, solitary
walkers, who, charity may suppose, were engaged in
deep and earnest converse with their own souls and

with heaven. In that large congregation there would
be some in mental darkness and distress, who would
instinctively and wisely seek to

> " Withdraw to haunts by man untrod,
> To hold communion there with God."

For, what Christian knows not that the secret sorrows
of the heart may not, and cannot, all be told to man?
There is sometimes a swelling tide of grief and sad-
ness in the soul that can only find an outflow heaven-
ward. Solitude is then sought, and it is peculiarly
sweet to those whose heart is greatly sin-grieved, as if
drowned in sorrow.

The graveyard, on Bar-hill, a little beyond and
above the town, was a favourite resort for not a few
during the "interval." It was very noticeable that the
strollers there, with but rare exceptions, were clad in
weeds of woe, and that their faces gave indication of
something more, and darker far, than a Sabbath
solemnity. Grief-worn features and wet eyes were to
be witnessed there. Numbers of the bereaved were
there, led thither not by idle curiosity but by affection,
for affection follows its objects even to the tomb.
Paradoxical as it seems, they were there to feed their
sorrow and to sip sepulchral solace; for there is a
strange, melancholy satisfaction felt on visiting the
resting place of the departed who were to us very dear.
A look at the grave of the loved gives vent to pent
up tears, and tends somehow to lighten the load of
grief that weighs on the heart. Such is the fact,

though psychological and physiological science may have failed to account for it.

In some part of that walled and somewhat extensive burial-ground might be seen, at the interval hour, on almost any summer Sabbath, standing beside a comparatively recent grave, a widow, with perhaps a child grasping her hand or holding timorously by her sable dress,—for the mother's hand had to be withdrawn from that of her child to wipe away the tears that began to trickle down her once rosy, but now pallid cheeks. There the widow and mother might be seen gazing fixedly and sadly on the sods that covered the earth-idol of her heart, the husband of her youth, and the father of her children. And if looks and heart-longings could bring the lost to life, he that lies in that tomb would soon be raised. But this cannot be! There he must lie, and there, despite his widow's grief and the world's turmoil, he will sleep full soundly till the resurrection morn, when all the dead shall spring to life, a mighty mass of immortality. Though doubtless well aware of this, yet still she looks, as if she saw or hoped to see, through the sward and mould, that face so loved and so familiar, which for years had been the light of her home and her heart. She looks, and looks, and heeds not others,— and others sacredly abstain from intrusion, lest they disturb her affectionate but sorrowful reverie. They steal quietly past at a respectful distance, and feel the while a thrill of pity pass through their bosoms. For the human heart is happily and delicately attuned to

C

sympathy, and the undulations of woe that are ever rolling across the graveyard fail not to cause the heart-cords of its living visitants to vibrate. Reader, have you never seen and felt what I here attempt feebly to describe ?

But other mourners beside the widow were there. Perchance a bereaved mother might be seen visiting the grave of her darling babe ; or that of her admired daughter cut down in the bloom of girlhood ; or that of her loved son who had been suddenly tumbled into the tomb just as manhood was about to crown his brow. We have long admired and wondered at the strength and durability of a mother's love, and fully and cordially assent to the affirmation of the poet when he says,

> " The warmest love that can grow cold,
> It is a mother's love."

No marvel that a mother's love should induce her to visit the tomb of her children, taken from her by the hand of God, through the instrumentality of disease or accident, when we know that a mother's love will cause her to cling to a prodigal son, to visit him in the prison cell, and to refuse to forsake him when he is dragged to the scaffold. The purity, the intensity, and undying character of a mother's affection, tell of the departure of a better state of things than the present, and point to a better world than this. How priceless a mother's affection, when guided by Christian principle and consecrated by Divine grace ! What a blessing to her family is a Christian mother.

Christian mothers are the best guarantee, next to Divine promise and power, for the future weal of our world ; and we are strongly inclined to believe that that power will be markedly exhibited, and these promises in large measure fulfilled, through the instrumentality of Christian mothers. Scripture and experience prove that as regards morality and religion, as well as arboreous nature, there is a truth and force in the aphorism, " As the twig is bent, the tree is inclined." But these remarks are intrusions here.

It could not escape the notice of an observant mind, that of those who visited the Bar-hill burying-ground, during the intermission of public worship on Sabbath, the great majority were *females*. And we suspect the same thing might be said of the unofficial voluntary visitants of churchyards. Why is it that, of those who go to muse and mourn among the tombs, the greater number are females? It seems to be woman's wont to go and weep by the grave of the loved. It has been so even with those cherishing the holiest, the most sanctified affection. It does seem, and to the honour of the sex be it said, that woman loves more ardently, more unselfishly, and more enduringly than man. And when her affection is hallowed by the baptism of the Spirit, it becomes a sublime and sacred passion, and most benign in its influences.

In my more juvenile years, Bar-hill was frequently

my resort on Sabbath, while worship was intermitted, and usually accompanied by some youth or youths of kindred spirit. It was no very sacred, and yet no unworthy motive that led me thither. I had no occasion then to go and mourn at the grave of a lost relative or friend. The churchyard of a neighbouring parish* gave grave-room to my forefathers and the more recent departed of my relatives. My visits were, perhaps, partly induced by a sort of sympathy with what was sad, to which I was no stranger, notwithstanding much blameable week-day frivolity; and probably also by the idea that there was great compatibility between the services of the Sabbath and the solemnity of the sepulchre.

But the chief attraction there to me was Peden's grave. There, at what was "the gallows fit," in Scotland's darkest days, that holy man Alexander Peden, the oracle of the west, found a resting place. He had been buried at the village of Auchinleck, about a mile and a half distant; but to do his remains dishonour, and to pour contempt on the sacred cause for which he lived and laboured, the persecuting and savage crew exhumed his body, and re-interred it, rudely enough, no doubt, at the foot of the gallows on Bar-hill at Cumnock. That was a sacred spot to me. Having read with avidity and deep interest the records of the labours and sufferings of the martyr-heroes of my native land, the grave of one of those men of

---

* New Cumnock.

whom the world was not then worthy, and whose memory was yet traditionally fragrant in the district, could not fail to have attractions for me; and every visit to such a spot deepened my detestation of oppression, which has never waned, and fanned in me the love of liberty, both civil and religious, a feeling which has only waxed, I ween, as years and intimacy with the world's wickedness have increased.

I loved to linger by Peden's grave. Well can I remember—and it is, perhaps, forty-five years ago— sitting on his broad tombstone and eating my Sabbath day "piece." The stone lay flat on the ground over the spot where the good man's body had been laid. It was then well worn by the feet of visitors, forming, as it did, the landing place inside from the jutting stone steps (or "style," as we called them) in the wall, and by which only access was obtained, except on funeral occasions, when the gate was opened. The "two thorns," spoken of in the Life of Peden, were there, the predicted junction of which is said to be fatal to Scotland—to drench the land in blood.

Few, if any, really believed Peden to be a prophet, a character that some have rashly claimed for him, but certainly all believed him to have been an eminently pious and devoted man, and a great sufferer for the cause of Christ.

It frequently happened that a number of families from a great distance assembled during the interval in one of the inns in the town, and had what was called a "refreshment," consisting of bread and cheese and

beer. From lack of light the ban of Christian society
did not then, as it happily in good measure does now,
rest on the sale and use of intoxicating drink. But I
never saw these Sabbath "refreshments" abused, and
often have I partaken of them. Some of the aged
Christian fathers were usually present, one of whom
asked a blessing by offering up a solemn prayer, and
another returned thanks, and the conversation was
invariably of a solemn and religious character. There
might be a little "bothering" and modest declining on
the part of some to say grace or return thanks, but
everything was conducted in a becoming and Christian-
like manner. There was no lightness, and least of all,
excess, which unsanctified genius has unfortunately
associated with these Sabbath reunions.

The hour of interval having expired, the worshippers re-assemble, and the services begin by
praise and prayer. There was no reading of Scripture, so far as I remember. But after prayer a few
lines were sung, and then the worthy minister gave
out the text. From that moment there was marked
stillness and attention, for his preaching was fitted to
rivet as well as to rouse. It was not a cold harangue,
or a compound of crudities. It consisted of vigorous
thinking and of earnest impassioned utterances. He
preached "as a dying man to dying men." It is said
that Dr John Dick, of Glasgow, than whom no one
was a better judge of preaching, paid Mr Wilson a
high compliment (and compliments were scarce with
the Doctor), after hearing him on some sacramental

occasion in the country. The Doctor simply remarked to some brother minister, and the remark is so like the Doctor, " That man can preach."

But I must close, and when I write again, I must speak of that memorable Sabbath Class in the Manse barn, and of the Sabbath evenings in my then loved and still gratefully remembered home.

IV.

THE MINISTER'S BIBLE CLASSES; SABBATH EVENING IN THE HOME.

IT is not yet forty years since Sabbath Schools and Bible Classes for the young were anything like common in the West of Scotland. At that date they were very rare in the district in which I resided, and I believe, with the exception perhaps of the cities and large towns, not many localities in the land were favoured with these excellent and much blessed nurseries of sacred knowledge and piety. As far as I am aware our worthy minister, Mr Wilson, was the first in that quarter of the country to institute classes specially for the religious instruction of the young. At what time he commenced this most important department of pastoral duty I know not; it was before my memory began to register matters of any moment; indeed, I am disposed to think it was at a date anterior to my day. He had two classes, one for those under twelve years of age, which met fort-nightly during the winter months and on a week day.

I can well remember, some forty-five or forty-six

years ago, trudging, not unwillingly, through mud
and mire, or snow-drift, as the case might be, on
every second Wednesday to the Meeting House at
Cumnock, a distance of five miles, to attend this
juvenile class. The exercises consisted in answering
a certain number of prescribed questions in " Brown's
Catechism," reciting (not reading) a portion of Scripture, and a Psalm in metre. Of course the exercises
were commenced and closed with prayer, and many
affectionate counsels were tendered in the interim by
the old and saintly man. The selections from
Scripture were varied, but chiefly from the writings
of David, and Solomon, and Isaiah, and John, and
Paul. At the end of the winter, when the class broke
up, each scholar, and the number was large, got some
little gift, such as a copy of Brown's Catechism,
Solomon's Proverbs, or the Proverbs and Psalms,
bound or stitched together. Suitable gift books of a
religious character for the young were neither so
abundant nor so easily procured then as they are now.
The money value of the books received might not be
great, but they were very highly valued ; if not for
the sake of their precious contents, they were greatly
prized for the sake of the donor.

Mr Wilson had a magic-like influence over the
young. He had a wonderful knack or readiness in
winning their confidence and affection ; though there
was nothing in his conduct of a fawning or feminine
character, but much that was markedly the reverse.
While he was open and frank to all, his temperament

was not a little irritable,—he could be angry and
rebuke to the face, and with great severity. Yet
despite this imperfection or failing he secured the
respect of all, the esteem of most, and effectually won
the affection of the young. There was about him a
warm-heartedness that nothing could cool, and a
gushing benevolence that no conduct on the part of
others could long or greatly interrupt. He was
sometimes angry, to his great grief, but I do believe
the sun never " went down on his wrath."

I remember an incident in connection with his
Wednesday class that indicated his tendency to
haste when provoked. As was to be expected in
such a large assemblage of children of all classes,
there were some rather rough boys who could scarcely
refrain from mischief, even when in class before the
minister. One such boy, on a certain occasion, had
been conducting himself with great impropriety in
some way ; on observing which, Mr Wilson instantly
reached over, and with his cane gave the wrong-doer
a very cordial crunt on the crown. This, no doubt,
made us all stand in awe and tremble. What was
said and done to the boy by the minister at dismissal
I do not recollect. But that the good man rested
content with what he had done I cannot believe. It
is more than probable that Master G——, at the
close of the class, would receive a sixpence, a kindly
pat on the head, and some kind words from the
minister. This boy's future course was in every sense
most creditable and successful. Long long years ago,

by his superior talents and good exemplary conduct, he won a most respectable position in the legal profession in the western metropolis of Scotland; and, if I mistake not, was and is, a leading man in one of that city's churches, adorning, I doubt not, the higher profession of the Christian.

How many are yet alive who belonged to that class in my time, I cannot tell. I suspect they are few. With most of them the day for work has closed, and night, workless night, has come! A solemn thought: and suggestive of the fact that my sun hies on to his setting, and cannot now be very far from his going down. All that sustains me in view of that event is a simple faith in the Gospel story, with which I was early made intellectually acquainted by revered and pious parents, and by Mr Wilson in his winter class for children. My desire and hope is that the young who may chance to read this, will value more and improve better than I did the precious opportunities of religious instruction enjoyed, and that they may rejoice all their days in the light of God's reconciled countenance.

Mr Wilson had another class for young persons from twelve to twenty-four years of age, which met during the summer months in the Manse barn on the afternoon of Sabbath, immediately after the close of public worship. To that class I was in due time transferred. And much connected therewith is yet fresh in memory as the events of yesterday. The aspect and utterances of that venerable man, and the

ardour and earnestness with which he instructed and
warned and wooed are not to be forgotten by those
who were privileged to see and hear him on these
deeply interesting occasions. All who survive will, I
am sure, join me in saying that these were gala days
as regarded advantage and enjoyment,—that they
take their place among "the greenest spots in
memory's waste."

Last summer, in a western district of the Province,
I met a farmer who had been a classmate of mine
under Mr Wilson, on these "lang syne" Sabbath
afternoons in the Manse barn at Bankhead, when,
unprompted by me, a tide of hallowed reminiscence
rose up in his mind, and he spoke in terms of grateful
and rapturous admiration of the man and of his
teachings. He seemed at a loss for language to
express his high estimate of both.

At the end of summer each year, when the class
closed, Mr Wilson after tendering suitable and affectionate counsel, cordially shook each scholar by the
hand on parting. These were sad and very solemn
scenes, and wet eyes were abundant, especially among
the female members of the class. None there so
hardened, or heedless and light-hearted as not to be
arrested, subdued, and melted by the farewell words
of that man of God. And that last parting with his
class in 1822,* I think, and not many months before

---

* This date does not fall under the heading of these notices, but the
reader will please forgive this transgression of prescribed bounds, as I
cannot well refrain.

he died, can neither be forgotten nor fully described. His health had been failing for some time. Disease was fast loosening the pins of his strong built earthly tabernacle. If I remember rightly he had frequently been assisted during that summer in the duties of the class by passing preachers, but specially by a worthy student, then on the eve of being licensed, and now an old and honoured minister to a large congregation in England, who too in his turn has for years required assistance in the onerous duties of his sacred calling.*

On the day the class was to close, Mr Wilson came into the barn, took his usual place on the floor, surrounded by his numerous and sorrowing young friends. He seemed conscious that the hand of death was on him, and addressed his eager sobbing auditors with all the earnestness and solemnity and authority of a dying man. It was an overpowering scene. The heart of the firmest palpitated and fluttered, and the eyes of those least given to weeping were wet. What would I give to hear again that farewell address, and to listen again to that parting prayer! But the wish is alike idle and foolish. It may, and must, suffice that the important and precious truths, then uttered by him, are all patent to me in God's blessed Word,—that the throne of grace which he then addressed, is as open and accessible to me and to others as it was to him, and that He who sits on that

---

* Probably the late Rev. Hugh Crichton, D.D., of Mount Pleasant, Liverpool, who died in 1871 in the forty-sixth year of his ministry.

throne is as ready to hear prayer now, as He was then.

Then came the last act, the parting scene, which was almost too much for affection to bear. Farewell, that saddest far of all vocables, must be said. The disease-stricken and death-doomed minister took his stand by the door and grasped the hand of each of his young friends as they passed out, imploring a blessing, or enunciating a Divine promise, or uttering some pointed Scriptural counsel. These last words of a loved teacher would linger in the ear and be treasured up in the memory, and may be supposed to have aided greatly in resisting temptation, and to have prompted strongly to the performance of duty in after life. The memory of that farewell scene and those farewell words, would be utterly incompatible with an after-life of sin and godless indifference.

There would no doubt be a sad heart in the manse that night; for severance from those held dear is a sore trial even to the saints. Grace neither destroys nor forbids feeling, but gives it purity and intensity,— yea, it converts love's delicate cords into cables, so that the heart holds and swings by the object of its affection even amid the throes of dissolution. The good dying minister could not but mourn separation from those he so sincerely loved, and whose spiritual interests he had so closely at heart. And well I wot there were young hearts truly sad that night in many of the dwellings of his people.

Perhaps, the reader will think that I have written

more than enough about these bygone matters of local
and sectional interest; and yet I would like to tell
something of how the Sabbath evening was spent in
my early home, in the hope that some heads of households may be induced to devote, more than heretofore,
the closing hours of the Lord's day to the religious
instruction of those whom God in his providence has
placed under their roof and specially committed to
their care. Parents and heads of households have
blessed opportunities given them of doing real and
permanent good to the rising race. And woe to those
whom Jehovah thus trusts and honours, if they are
unfaithful stewards of this great grace. Will not the
blood of many children and servants be required at
the hands of their parents and masters? I fear it will
be even so; for who knows not, that neglect of
domestic instruction in Divine things, is one of the
most common and clamant crimes in this our day?
Both God and men expect that parents will give to
their children the first and most important lessons in
religion.

And it is not to be denied that home is the best
school of divinity, — provided parents are what
they should be, viz., pious, familiar with the Bible,
and duly faithful. I think I am free to say that I
learned more real divinity at my father's fireside than
afterwards in the halls of learning, or from all the
books I have since read and studied. For this I can
claim no credit, as, to my great responsibility, and I
much fear to my great guilt, I was favoured with the

tutorage of a parent more skilled than most in sacred lore.

But it is not great gifts, or great acquirements in religious knowledge that are needed to the faithful and profitable discharge of parental duty to the young. If parents were only truly pious, they could and would teach their children that which would avail them infinitely more than world's wealth. It is astonishing how much and how effectively a real Christian can teach even though illiterate in the world's acceptation of the term. Even he "who" experimentally "knows his Bible true, and knows no more" can do much, very much, to instruct the young in those things that concern their everlasting peace.

It was my inestimable privilege in youth to be a member of a family in which a goodly portion of the evening of every Sabbath was specially devoted to religious instruction. After returning from the public services of the day, and the evening meal over, every one able to read took up some suitable and congenial book, of which there was no lack either for Sabbath-day or week-day reading. Several of the religious magazines of the day were also available, and were greedily devoured by the elder branches of the family. Missionary intelligence, then not so rife as now, was greatly relished. I may remark there was seldom much conversation indulged in on Sabbath in the family, and none whatever was allowed of a worldly or trifling character. Any unnecessary allusion to country news or secular matters was instantly checked, and the erring one solemnly and severely reproved.

Reading and silence usually continued till about eight o'clock, when the head of the house ordered the books to be put aside and all the members of the family to be called. Then he put to each a question from the Assembly's Shorter Catechism, and proceeded thus round and round till the half of the Catechism was gone over. It was an invariable rule to make the Fifth Commandment the point of division; all the questions before it on one Sabbath evening, and all after it to the end on the next Sabbath evening,—so that the whole Catechism was gone over every two weeks. This exercise, chiefly of the memory, being finished, some doctrine was taken up and investigated in the light of Scripture with great minuteness and much logical acumen. The catechist comprehended as fully, and could evolve and elucidate as clearly, the glorious mysteries of the Christian faith as any whose words I have heard, or whose writings I have read. In theology he had read extensively, I believe nearly all the principal works then extant on Divinity in the English language, and had thought closely, and was thus well fitted to be an instructor in sacred things.

This estimate of his knowledge and powers was not limited to those who might be swayed by partiality to a parent. The excellent pastor under whose ministry he sat during the latter years of his life, once stated to me that he was indebted to him for consistent and satisfactory views of one of the most difficult of Divine doctrines. And some of the better-informed adherents of the kirk (to which in early life he belonged), wondered and regretted that "such a sensible man should be a seceder," little dreaming that it was just his sense or knowledge, conjoined with high unflinching conscientiousness, that constrained him to leave the State-fenced fold, and to cast in his lot with those followers of Christ, who sought no patronage from civil power, and who scorned with holy horror the intrusion of secular authority into the household of faith.

These catechetical exercises on Sabbath evening were of the most instructive character, deserving and demanding the attention, and not seldom heavily taxing the reflective powers of the catechumens. There was no tolerance for inattention or indifference, and scant enough patience with those who manifested anything like obtuseness of mind. Perceiving clearly himself, the examiner seemed to think (which was only very human) that others should discover the relations and results of doctrines as readily and vividly as he did. The rebukes at times administered for inattention, or unthoughtful stupid answers, were of crushing character and not easily forgotten. Though constitutionally kind and generally considerate, his authority was towering and imperative. Alas for the victim of his few but withering words of merited rebuke. And yet these words did not excite enmity or ill will, though assuredly they humbled and profoundly deepened respect for him who uttered them.

Though doctrines were the staple in these Sabbath evening instructions, yet their application — their influence on the heart and life—were not neglected. Toward the close there were usually questions put and remarks made about practical and personal religion, that not unfrequently caused some of us to keep our eyes fastened on the floor the while, lest they should meet the keen searching glance of our earthly parent,—aware that we were spiritually far from what we should be, and, I trust, wished to be. "Conscience makes cowards of us all!" I can yet almost feel the burning blush that must then have mantled my face when some close pressing question about personal piety was put to me. And that blush might not ill-befit me even at this late day of my life; for I have to say with far more painful truth than he who first employed the words, "I have not attained, neither am I yet perfect." But I do desire to follow after, &c.

After putting a few simple questions, and tendering some good advice to the mere juveniles of the house-hold, and hearing them repeat the Lord's Prayer and the Creed, and the verses of the psalm and chapter committed to memory during the day, the "big ha' Bible" was taken down and opened, and family worship engaged in as usual, only, if possible, with a deeper solemnity, induced by engagement in the services of the sanctuary and the immediately preced-ing exercises in the family. After reading the verses of the psalm to be sung, a short prayer was offered up for Divine aid in worship,—a most becoming practice,

and one that I like exceedingly, though through the
influence of current Christian custom, I have in
general dispensed with it, but not with the entire
approbation of my own mind. The psalm on Sabbath
evening was generally sung to some plaintive air,
such as Coleshill, and the exercise was peculiarly
sweet and solemn. The father's manly but not
unmusical voice guiding and blending with the voices
of the large family God had given him,—some of
them mere children, and others often men and women
grown, constituted music to the mind and to the ear
worth learning and remembering, and which I doubt
not was graciously heard in heaven. Suppose that
psalm coming in course on a Sabbath evening, and it
is by no means unlikely, which says—

> "But unto them that do Him fear
> God's mercy never ends;
> And to their children's children still
> His righteousness extends."

Would not these words, if sung in strong faith, by the
parents and the children, prove a solace and security
in view of the dark and unknown future ? Well they
might, for they convey a precious promise, the fulfil-
ment of which is too seldom remarked, and at best
but ungratefully enjoyed. The worship-song of that
family yet lingers in my ear. Its like, in all respects,
I cannot hope to hear again. The psalm being sung,
a passage of Scripture was read, and then prayer,
solemn, earnest prayer was offered for a blessing on
the services of the day,—for the sealing of God's word

savingly on the mind and heart of all who had heard or read it,—for the extension of Christ's Kingdom and the building up of Zion. And, oh, how the father and the priest wrestled in prayer for the salvation and guidance of all his family and household. If one of that numerous family is at last unsaved, it will not be for want of instruction and counsel and example and prayer on the part of their parents... No! the hands of their parents will be found clean of their souls' blood.

Thus was spent and thus was closed the Sabbath evening in the privileged and happy home of my youth. Would that the meridian of my life had been, and that now its evening-time might be, worthy of its favoured dawn—its singularly privileged morning.

I beg to add one remark about Sabbath evenings at home; viz., that though the sermons heard during the day were very frequently talked over in the evening, and a statement of the "heads and particulars" required of some of us, yet I never heard the guidman find fault with the preacher or utter a word depreciatory either of his talents or orthodoxy. And any captious or carping remark made by any of us youngsters in our fastidiousness and folly was instantly and peremptorily frowned down, and our dissatisfaction referred to our ignorance or to our evil hearts.

Reader, when I intrude on you again it will be to speak of a Communion Sabbath in the olden time.

V.

COMMUNION SABBATH.

A COMMUNION SABBATH, with previous and subsequent services, constituted a semi-annual era of singularly solemn and memorable interest in my early days,—so much so that I sometimes feel inclined to conclude that "the former days were better than these"—that more of heavenly unction distinguished the Christianity of our fathers than can be claimed for ours—that, in special, sacramental seasons with them were of a more hallowed character than with us. At the same time, I am well aware that this sentiment or opinion, which not unfrequently obtrudes itself on me, may be indebted for much of its force, if not for its very existence, to the searing and deadening influence which years have exerted on my feelings. However, that influence, if I am capable of judging, has not been great, as I still feel youthful and fresh of heart, though my head, alas, gives indubitable indications of age.

But, let the case be as it may, one thing is certain, viz.; that the sacramental solemnities witnessed by me in the days of yore, in the west of Scotland, constitute at this distant day "green spots on memory's waste," and I firmly believe were Bethel scenes and seasons of high and holy enjoyment to many of God's people, of whom not a few have long ago fallen asleep in Jesus, and some "remain unto this present."

The church assembling in the Meeting House at Cumnock celebrated the Lord's Supper twice a year, viz., about mid-summer, and again in the dead of winter. The services on these occasions were much alike. The only distinction noteworthy, regarded the place where the extra-Meeting House sermons were preached. On the summer sacramental Sabbath, while the communion services were going forward in the house, three or four sermons were preached in the open air on a beautiful Green in the immediate vicinity. But at the winter sacrament, strange to say, the Parish Kirk was kindly granted, after morning service, and I believe was better filled, and honoured with better gospel preaching, on such occasions, than on any Sabbath all the year round. A sort of heartless humdrum morality constituted the staple of State-paid preaching in that and in many other kirks in Scotland at that period. It is said things have changed for the better in this respect. Thanks to the provocation of secession and dissent, which has saved from absolute rottenness the Ecclesiastical Establishments of Britain; though little gratitude is felt, and less expressed, for this important service.

Some of the aged, who were privileged to spend their youth in some corner of Scotland where the religious element predominated, will bear me out in saying that the coming sacrament threw its solemn shadow over days and weeks before. Conduct, which at other times might be indulged in, not being deemed in itself sinful, though bordering on levity or unlicensed enjoyment, was watchfully avoided as the communion season drew on. The walk became more careful. Mirth and everything that savoured of jollity were abjured and banned in view of the pending solemnity.

For a good while previous, those that were candidates for the Church membership had weekly interviews with the minister,—interviews calculated to leave a deep, serious impression on their minds. They, in general, walked not only circumspectly, but tenderly, apparently bearing in mind "the dying of the Lord Jesus." And as the time drew near, intending communicants, even those who lived most closely with God, began, as it were, to gather up their skirts—to "gird up the loins of their minds," as their mental and spiritual habitudes, as might be expected, had been less or more loosened, and, may be, had got a little *draigled* amid the toil and moil of this trying world. They began betimes to make ready for the right and profitable observance of the feast, by more frequent searchings of heart, by more earnestness in prayer, and by a more careful walk before the Lord, if not before those that were without. Preparation-work began early, and it became more earnest, and assumed more of outwardness, if not of actuality, as the solemn season approached.

The Sabbath preceding was termed, by way of distinction, the "Preparation Sabbath." Nor was this designation inappropriate, as the services in the sanctuary had more or less of special reference to the sacramental work of the following Sabbath. Then Thursday or Friday was set apart for self-examination and humiliation. It was called, though not with much propriety or truth, the "Fast Day," as few, if any, literally fasted thereon. Still, as I know, some conscientiously partook but sparingly on that day of "the bread that perisheth,"—not more than was deemed necessary to sustain nature under the rather long journey to and from the house of God.

I would here observe that fasting is at times an important religious duty, and, then, when voluntarily, conscientiously, and cordially observed, cannot fail to be acceptable to God, and profitable to the soul. But periodical and statutory fasts, whether appointed by the Church or the State, are of more than doubtful character. Is there not ground to fear that such enactments have well nigh brought the religious duty of fasting into contempt? Yet there are many amongst us who ought to know better and to act otherwise, not satisfied with God's authority to fast, seek, and are impiously fain to have governmental authority for their abstinence, their humiliation, and their thanksgiving. Would that all such reflected on the following interrogatory and inspired statement,— "Know ye not, that to whom ye yield yourselves servants to obey, his servants ye are to whom ye

obey?" As regards Christian duties, Christians
should know no king but Jesus. Alas! some there
are who divide with another their allegiance to Him,
though, in charity, we must suppose they wot it not.
These remarks may seem to some out of place in this
narrative, but they are not uncalled for in Canada.

On the sacramental fast day two sermons were
preached by one or two of the assistant ministers.
And at the close of the service, after earnest prayer
for Divine direction, tokens of admission to the table
of the Lord on the coming Sabbath were distributed
to the members, which, in the case of not a few, were
evidently received with much fear and trembling.
The congregation again assembled for worship on
Saturday, when two sermons were usually preached.
By this time all the ministers who were to assist on
the occasion had arrived. Of such there were usually
three and sometimes four. And it was no season of
idleness or ease with them. Ample work was found
for them all on Sabbath.

After the dismissal of the congregation on Saturday,
the members of the church carefully and kindly
invited to their homes those who had come up from
neighbouring congregations to celebrate with them
the death of their common Lord. In those days it
was common for many of the really and devotedly
pious, who could at all command the time, to attend
communions in the surrounding country, in some
cases at great distances from their homes. For such
an object the time spent was deemed no loss, and

the toil of travel was estimated lightly. Love to Christ and desire of fellowship with Him in His appointed ordinance of the Supper make long roads short and rough roads smooth. When a mere boy I have walked and run many miles early of a Saturday morning to bring back the horse that bore so far on his way, to a distant communion scene, a near and deservedly revered relative. Well do I remember the terror experienced, while returning from one of these sacred errands, on being overtaken, far from home and in a strange part of the country, by a terrible thunder storm, and having in charge a restive animal, which my then puny arm was ill able either to restrain or guide. The interchange of sentiment and the reciprocation of affection, at these sacramental seasons, by Christians residing far apart, but then brought together, were very pleasant and, no doubt, very profitable. There is no friendship so holy, so close and endearing as that cherished by those who hold a common faith and a common hope. The communion of saints is too little cultivated, and seems to be but ill understood.

On the sacramental Sabbath morning the members of the church who dwelt at a distance had to be very early astir, not merely because worship commenced at the Meeting House an hour earlier than usual, viz., at ten o'clock, but also because there were sacred duties, in some measure peculiar to that day, demanding their attention in the morning; such as re-examination of their spiritual state—of their faith and love and obedience. And there was a felt need for special and earnest prayer that grace might be granted for the solemn work which the day was to witness.

I think there was more attention paid to heart-preparation for communion work by Christians of those days than by the generality of professors now. The commemoration of Christ's death was deemed, and rightly, an act of worship and of covenant engagement of the most august, important, and critical character. And, verily, there is no hypocrisy more dishonouring to the Saviour or more damaging to the soul,—no forswearing more criminal, more searing, or more sad than that of which those are guilty who sit down at the table of the Lord, fully conscious that their hearts are alienated from God and from Christ, and destitute of all desire for reconciliation. This is to lie to the Lord at His own table! No wonder that He should be angry. Well might Paul warn professing Christians of the guilt and danger of " eating and drinking unworthily."

True believers may often have fears,—may have a faith so feeble that they can only touch the hem of Christ's garment instead of grasping Him with giant grip, as His word warrants, and yet their hearts may be leal and loving the while, and they may be welcome and favoured guests at His table. We believe that Christ is never dishonoured by, or displeased with, those at His table who have been drawn thither by the cords of love and impelled by

His authority,—who are there from a desire to love
and honour Jesus, no matter how feeble their faith,
or how great their fears may be. The Son of God
is never "trodden under foot" by those who trembling,
approach His table. Inasmuch as it is in their heart
to do Him honour, He will not spurn them away, no,
nor hide His face from them, nor allow them to leave
unblessed.

As ten of the clock approaches numbers are pouring
in from the country, not only those who are wont to
come thither to worship, but strangers as well, many
on foot, some on horseback, some in carts, and a few
in more comfortable conveyances. And the towns-
folk begin to move in family groups with silent
tread toward the Meeting House and the adjoining
Green, the centre to which all tend on this sacramental morn. It was an interesting sight, similar
I ween, though in miniature, to that which the
approaches to Jerusalem, and the precincts of the
Temple, exhibited of old when the tribes of Israel
went up to celebrate one or other of the great annual
festivals. And surely there are many of God's true
Israel among those who are wending their way, on
this festival morning, to the house of God. The
members enter the Meeting House, and as many of
the adherents as the place will hold,—perhaps about
a thousand, when the passages as well as the pews
were filled. The remaining multitude gathered
around the tent on the Green, seating themselves
on the grass, or on chairs and stools and planks,

previously placed there, or, which was not uncommon nor counted unseemly, carried in the hands or borne on the shoulders of the worshippers as they came up.

In the church the worship began at ten precisely. There was, if possible, a greater solemnity than usual pervading the assembly. The stillness was intense. And the eagerness of eye and ear was very observable. All seemed conscious of their nearness to God,—that they were in the very "gate of heaven," and about to address themselves to a work, than which there can be none more sacred engaged in by man on this side of the Jordan of death, viz., the commemoration of the death of God's Son in the room of sinners. And the minister, Mr Wilson, seemed to feel a hallowed influence more than ordinary. There was singular unction even in the reading of the psalm, and still more in the prayer that followed the swelling song of praise sent up by that great congregation. And in the sermon—the action sermon it was called—he grew in earnestness and eloquence till he bordered on the region of rapture, and spoke like a man inspired.

The text chosen, on such an occasion, was usually one that led him directly to the garden of Gethsemane, or to the hill of Calvary, or to the tomb of Joseph of Arimathea, or to the Mount of Olives by Bethany. And oh, with what power and pathos he discoursed of the love, and sufferings and death of the Lord Jesus. "Christ crucified for our sins" constituted less or more of the theme of his preaching on every Sabbath, but on the communion Sabbath it might be said to have

been the beginning, the middle, and the ending of his
sermon,—it was throughout Christ's dying love. And
what attention and interest the sermon excited! There
might be, and doubtless were, agitated bosoms, and
moist eyes might be witnessed, but a sleeper or even
a listless look you had searched for in vain.

After the action sermon came "the fencing of the
tables," a discourse of considerable length, in which
the minister endeavoured to point out who were
worthy, and who were not worthy, to take their seats
at the Lord's table. This part of the service, when
judiciously performed, was highly beneficial in comforting those of tender conscience and encouraging
the timid, and also in warning the presumptuous, the
self-righteous, and the immoral. As far as memory
serves, I think Mr Wilson discharged this duty wisely
and well. He was a man of large heart, and of tender
Christ-like sympathies, and could, by the grace of his
Divine Master, "comfort the cast down." But it has
been my lot to hear table fencings of most objection-
able—of most unchristian character. I have heard
ministers so fence the Lord's table, by placing the
ten commandments in every avenue leading to it,
that, had not intending communicants known more of
the pardoning mercy and rich grace of God to the
guilty, than the ministers seemed to do, the Lord's
table would have been left without a single guest.
Cautions and warnings and aids to examination are
necessary and all-important. But these should be
given in the spirit of the gospel, and in accordance

with Scripture, and at some time convenient previous
to the dispensation of the Supper. It is by no means
a suitable time to debar, when the communicants have
already received tokens and are seated at the table.

The work of communicating commenced when the
fencing was finished, and after the Scripture warrant
for observing the ordinance was read. There were
two long narrow tables in front of the precentor's
desk, covered with snow-white linen, at which the
communicants took their seats. These tables would
accommodate rather more than fifty persons at a time.
The patriarchal elders gravely walked round the
tables, taking up the tokens from the parties seated
thereat. And Mr Wilson, the minister of the church,
addressed and served the first table, speaking from
ten to fifteen minutes before distributing the elements,
and about the same length of time after : so that each
table service occupied from twenty-five to thirty
minutes.

The remaining table services, usually amounting to
fourteen (the membership was over 700) were conducted by the assistant ministers in rotation, some of
them addressing, perhaps, four or five tables or sets of
communicants. Between each table service a few
verses of a Psalm, either the 103rd or 105th, were sung,
and all but invariably to the good old solemn air of
Coleshill, a tune which this and other sacred, as well
as sad, associations have hallowed in my estimation.
I cannot but revere it apart from the merit of its
music, having in youth heard it sung, year after year,

by the great congregation round the communion
table, and oftener still by a happy household around
the holiest family altar at which it was ever mine to
worship; and not unfrequently have I heard it
chaunted by the dying saint and the grief-stricken
group around his bed.

While communion work was proceeding in the
Church, and it usually continued till near seven o'clock
at night, sermon after sermon was being preached
from the tent to listening hundreds on the Green.
There was no intermission of the service either without or within doors; but there was often a good deal
of movement between the Church and the Green as
some popular minister transferred his services from
the one place to the other, and a great many found it
necessary to retire into the town for a short time,
for refreshment, during the day. But I am not aware
that any unseemly conduct attended this. Seceder
sacraments were not suitable scenes for excess even
with the godless, who attended the out-door preaching.
At these, the spiritual influences were too strong to
allow of such.

When the communion services had closed in the
church, Mr Wilson addressed those who had been
at the table, and especially those who had been there
for the first time. These were the objects of his
anxious solicitude. These addresses were very
memorable; they were so parental, so tender, and so
earnest. How he warned against the temptations of
the world, the deceitfulness of the heart, and the wiles

E

of Satan! Thus closed services than which I have never witnessed any that exceeded in solemnity and heavenly character. No doubt to multitudes it was an high day of holy enjoyment, strengthening them greatly for their future work and warfare, enabling them to "go on their way rejoicing."

I must remark, for the purpose of showing the great superiority of simultaneous over sectional communion, that there was often uncomfortable and very unseemly crowding and elbowing to get forward to the tables. I have seen it a perfect jam from the entrance to the tables, all along the passes, and even to the outside of the door, and that for hours and hours—many having to remain thus pent up during two or three table services, only being carried forward a little as each table was dismissed. Such a position was very trying for the aged and the feeble, especially females. And what was worse, poor human nature was sometimes like to rebel. Those who had strong tempers and weak graces could hardly bear with their brethren who innocently trod on their toes or squeezed their sides. And there was reason to fear that there were sometimes silent physical repulsions not of the gentlest character. The arrangement was anything but wise, unavoidably causing bodily discomfort and mental distraction, when about to engage in a most solemn and sacred service. Communicating simultaneously in the pews is a manifest and great improvement, and now obtains in all churches whose affairs are conducted judiciously.

At the conclusion of the pastor's address to those who had communicated, to which I have already alluded, prayer was offered up, and a portion of a psalm sung, after which the whole congregation retired to the Green, where the closing sermon was preached, usually by one of the ablest and most acceptable of the assistant ministers. The audience now was very large. I have seen numbers of the loafers and godless gentry of the town listening in groups at the outskirts of the crowd. The evening sermon was often of striking and stirring character, and remembered and spoken of long after. The preacher no doubt went up well prepared. And the opportunity was the best the day afforded for proclaiming the gospel, at least as far as numbers were concerned. It afforded a fine opportunity, such as an apostle would have hailed and improved. I have no doubt many souls were brought to Christ, and many built up in Christ on that lovely Green. Many, many a glorious gospel sermon was preached there.

It was, I think, in one of these sacramental evening sermons at Cumnock, preached by Dr James Hall of Edinburgh, who had in former years been minister of the congregation, that I first heard of Heber's beautiful missionary hymn, commencing with the lines—

"From Greenland's icy mountains,
From India's coral strand."

The Doctor quoted the hymn with great effect, toothless as he then was. I believe it had been but recently published. Its beauty arrested the attention

of some who heard it from the lips of the Doctor.
He was applied to for a copy. From that time it
became a familiar and a favourite in the quarter, and
perhaps tended to awaken and cherish a missionary
spirit in more than one individual. The singing of
the psalm at the close, by such a multitude in the
open air, as the sun was sinking beneath the horizon,
and the faint shades of a summer's evening threaten-
ing soon to descend, had a strangely subduing and
soothing effect on the mind. Some of my readers,
who have listened to a worship-song by a vast
assembly in the open air as evening set in, must have
felt, what lack of utterance prevents me describing.

The benediction was pronounced, and the work of
the day ended. The worshippers retire and proceed
to their homes, musing, we may charitably suppose,
on what they had that day heard of the word of life,
and done out of love to their Lord, and in obedience
to His command. And would not thanksgiving
ascend that night from many a closet and many a
family altar for the privileges and enjoyments of such
a day. What would I give to enjoy again one such
day! But ah! I am now far from the place where,
and the time when such a day as I have attempted to
describe, was last witnessed and enjoyed by me.
Small likelihood there is that I shall ever again see
the sacred spot, and I dare not even hope to witness a
similar scene, or one in all respects to me so deeply
interesting.

VI.

THANKSGIVING MONDAY.

IN those days, the services connected with a Sacramental season did not close with the Sabbath. The congregation assembled again on Monday to give thanks for the special privilege enjoyed on the previous day, and for the forbearance exercised in not "mingling their blood with their sacrifice." And also, as was most meet, for presenting earnest prayer that forgiveness might be granted for the sins committed, through ignorance or otherwise, "in the holy things of the Lord." The best of God's people are painfully conscious that great imperfection pertains to them, tainting their purest deeds, and marring the acceptability of their sacred services. There is a felt need of pardon,—of being "sprinkled with the much incense" of the Redeemer's righteousness, even when rising from His table, and withdrawing from His presence-chamber. And the more enlightened in spiritual matters, and the more advanced in the divine life, the more forcibly is the need of forgiveness felt by believers,—a fact that is fatal to the theory held by some, that perfection is attainable on this side heaven.

On the thanksgiving Monday the people met

around the tent on the Green, where they had waited
and worshipped till a late hour the evening before.
The multitude was not so very large as on Sabbath ;
still it was a large assembly, and a goodly sight to
see so many of all classes and of all ages assembled to
worship God under the open canopy of heaven. The
distinctions that obtain in secular and social life did
did not there obtrude to foster pride in one, and
excite envy in another. Those " in goodly apparel "
sat ungrudgingly side by side with those habited in
hodden and russet. Superior place or position was
sought by none. Landlord and tenant, master and
servant, occupied alike humbly the high and honour-
able position of worshippers—a position not only the
most becoming, but the most exalted that a man
can occupy on earth or in heaven. Many family
groups might be observed in that promiscuous
assembly ; some of them embracing three, if not four
generations. Near to, and under, the watchful eye of
the mother, were the playful and prattle-loving
youngsters. Around were seated the elder born,
some of them " men and women grown ;" and close by,
might be seen seated the venerated grandsire, his body
bent, his face furrowed and his head " silvered o'er
with years."

To a close observer there was something markedly
different in the facial aspect of the worshippers, from
that which met the eye on the previous days of
the solemnity. This remark refers almost exclusively
to those who had been communicants. On the fast

day, and on Saturday, and especially on the Sabbath, their looks indicated awe and anxiety, and in some cases fear. On Monday their features, on which the flags of feeling were hung out, told of calm content within—of gratitude, and even of gladness. All this can be easily accounted for without attributing any portion of it, as some would, to superstition, or self-righteousness, or vile hypocrisy. On the previous days they were approaching, and about to engage in, a very solemn and important work,—a work on the right performance of which depended the honour of the Saviour, and the weal of their own souls. And, as in duty bound, they were no doubt earnestly engaged in the painful business of self-examination, letting the clear light of God's Word fall on their past path. And would there not be discovered, even in the case of the best of them, more than sufficient of sins and short-comings to prompt penitent sorrow, and to sadden the countenance. Nor would this be all. The work of self-examination would be but half performed were we to stop short with a mere survey, however careful, of our past conduct, without regard to our present con-dition. There must be a fearless and full inspection of our desires and motives, the secret springs of our actions. And who is the man that can feel, and smile, complacency, after a rigid scrutiny of the arcana of his heart with the lamp of God in his hand? That man dwells not on this side the Jordan of death. There is more than enough of lingering depravity in the holiest heart, when revealed by the Word and

Spirit of God, to flood that heart with grief, and to shroud the face in gloom.

No wonder then that intending communicants, being engaged in the solemn work of self-examination, should exhibit deep anxiety or even fear. Self-jealousy is perfectly compatible with faith in Jesus Christ. Its very existence is an indication of love. Is it asked, Why the altered state of feeling and of feature on the Monday from what they had been on the previous days of the solemnity? Why! because an imperative command had been obeyed, an important duty had been performed, a precious privilege had been enjoyed;—the table of the Lord had been approached, and no judgment had fallen on the guests gathered there;—no such startling question had been put, as " Friends, how came you in hither, not having wedding garments?" and consequently there had been no such dread mandate given, as " Bind them hand and foot and take them away, and cast them into outer darkness." All which would be taken as a token for good—that their service had been accepted by Him who had said, " Do this in remembrance of me." And may we not with much confidence suppose that many, if not all, had been enabled by faith to receive the words of Christ as addressed to them, " Be of good cheer, your sins are forgiven you." And would there not be a felt resting on Christ at His table—a going out of the heart's affections towards their Redeemer while celebrating His death in their law-room ?

Such being the case, it had indeed been strange if, on assembling for thankgiving on Monday, their hearts had not felt glad, and if their faces had not shone, irradiated by the spiritual joy within. Why, they were reaping a portion of that great reward that infallibly accrues to those that keep God's command-ments. Has not the Christ-loving reader often felt a sweet satisfaction, and experienced pure pleasure after the discharge of important duty, and after the enjoy-ment of a precious privilege? The disciples will ever be glad when they see the Lord. And where is He to be met with, if not in the path of duty? Where is He to be seen, if not at His own table?

It was very apparent that the Monday after the Sac-rament was a day of light-heartedness, and calm quiet joy, with the mass of worshippers. But we dare not deny that there might be some in that large assembly whose joy was illegitimate. Perhaps there were some who felt glad because relieved of the pressure and re-straint caused by such solemn services, and foolishly supposed that they were at liberty for a time to live very much as they might list. If such there were, it is to be hoped the number was small.

The services of the day were conducted by two of the assistant ministers. Each preached a sermon. As far as I remember the discourses on these occasions were in general very much what sermons should be, viz., redolent of Gospel truth, less or more instructive, admonitory and comforting. It sometimes happened that novel and knotty subjects were discussed by

ministers of somewhat eccentric minds. I remember
of hearing propounded, on one of these sacramental
occasions, very singular views in regard to the millennium by a worthy but rather eccentric minister, the
Rev. Mr. Monteath of Moffat, which caused a great
deal of after-talk and discussion among the people.
His bodily vision was then almost if not altogether
gone, at least it was said he had the wrong end of the
psalm book to him when he read or repeated the
psalm ;* but his mental vision appeared to be clear
and vigorous ; he seemed to look with great ease
and confidence along the line of prophecies far into
the future. But some of his brethren thought he
sometimes tried to look farther than prophetic dicta
indicated or allowed. However this might be, I am
inclined to think that his theories in regard to the
millennium, for which we should all look and long,
were just as near the truth as most of those propounded in these later days.

In some churches, immediately before my day, the
Monday of the Sacrament was specially devoted to
polemical preaching—to "riding the marches" between
truth and error. It was by many deemed a duty on
that day not only to defend their own creed, but to
assail and denounce other creeds in as far as they ran
counter to, or infringed on, orthodoxy, as defined by
the assailants. It fared hard with Popery and Prelacy,
and as many of the heterodox "isms" as time per-

---

* He was almost blind before he was settled.

mitted to be brought under the ecclesiastical flail. I
have heard rather a racy story told, in this connection,
of the Rev. Mr Robertson of Kilmarnock, a man
eminent for moral worth and piety, and distinguished
above his fellows for vigour of intellect and vast
acquirements ; but who, for a good while, was subjected to considerable aberration of mind, a calamity
from which, in the mysterious providence of God, the
most gifted of gospel heralds are not exempted. Who
that reads this will not recall to mind the repeated
eclipse that came over the gigantic intellect of the
saintly Robert Hall of Leicester? Mr Robertson, I
believe, in great measure recovered from this sad
affliction, though I rather think his mind never
entirely regained its normal tone. However, he felt
it to be a duty, as it was his delight, to preach ; and it
was said he could preach with great power.

On a certain occasion, as the story goes, he was
assisting the Rev. Dr Pringle, of Perth, and it fell to
his lot to preach on the Monday after the Communion.
It was well known that Mr Robertson was a hearty
hater of error, and especially of Popish errors. The
Doctor and his brother, who were present, were afraid
—and not without cause—that he would overdo the
customary "threshing"; that he would violate good
taste and exceed the bounds of Christian propriety in
castigating the Roman Catholics when their turn
came. It was deemed necessary to adopt some means
to secure, if possible, moderation, at least as regarded
length, to the denunciations of Popery and Papists, by

Mr R.   So, at breakfast, the Doctor addressed Mr R.
to the following purport :—" It's usual on this day to
point out the leading errors o' the age, and, nae doubt,
the Papists are a' wrang ; but a' folk ken that we
dinna like or approve o' Popery, so there is nae need
for your sayin' muckle about it the day.   And should
ye forget, and continue owre lang on the subject, I'll
gang wi' ye to the pu'pit and sit ahint ye, and when
ye hae said eneugh, I'll just gie yer coat-tail a wee bit
pu', and then ye ken it's time to stop."

This arrangement was tolerated, it would seem, by
the party addressed, for the Doctor did go to the pulpit,
and took his seat behind the preacher.   As expected, Mr
Robertson, in his sermon, dragged Popery to the bar,
and treated it and its professors without ceremony and
without mercy.   The subject, as usual, roused him : he
waxed more and more vehement, no doubt transfixing
his opponents with arguments, and covering them
with denunciations, when the Doctor gave his coat-tail
a gentle tug.   On this, Mr R. reined in, and proceeded
to say, apologetically, that had time permitted, he
would have shown, from Scripture and from reason,
that Popery was this, so and so bad, and that bad ;
and on and on he went, till he became as excited and
as scathing as before, when the Doctor gave his coat-tail
another and more emphatic tug.   This again arrested
and calmed him for a little.   But he would not thus,
or yet, give it up, but proceeded, as before, to say that
had time allowed, he would have shown that Popery
was, &c., &c. ; and on he rushed again till he reached,

if possible, a higher height of fury, flinging unsparingly the bolts of argument at the vile system, and pouring on it a very torrent of anathemas. The Doctor could bear it no longer, so he gave his coat-tails a third and harder pull than either of the preceding ; when lo! Mr R. turned hurriedly round in the pulpit, and addressing the Doctor, who had been kindly acting as his monitor, said, " What are ye pu'ing at ? I'll denounce the Catholics though you and a' the deevils in hell were pu', pu'ing at ma tails." What followed this ridiculous, yet painful scene, I never heard. It would, no doubt, aid in bringing into desuetude a practice utterly unsuited to a Sacramental season.

As far back as I can remember, there was no such formal assault on errors and errorists made by the preachers on Sacramental Mondays at Cumnock ; and it was mine to hear, then and there, not a few ministers of the olden school, who proved themselves sturdy polemics, and were ready to " contend earnestly for the faith once delivered to the saints," when error threatened its stability in the minds of the people. But it was not often they put themselves to the trouble of re-slaying the slain. Their aim as well as their effort was to hold up and commend " the truth as it is in Jesus" to the acceptance of their hearers. This is the great business of the gospel minister. It is by " holding forth the Word of Life" that sinners are converted, and the saints edified. Still, every good minister of Jesus Christ will equip himself for contest, as best he may, by study, and storing his mind with varied knowledge, and be ready at the call of duty to enter the lists and do battle in behalf of sacred truth.

It would be to me a somewhat pleasing task to jot down reminiscences of the many worthy ministers that assisted at Communions in the congregation at Cumnock during the years of my boyhood. But such jottings would be uninteresting and profitless to others. These " good and faithful servants " have nearly all, and many of them long years ago, entered into the joy of their Lord. Only one, I think, remains, who assisted during the ministry of my first and much revered pastor, Mr Wilson. And that one was then a young minister, and Mr Wilson had nearly concluded his work in the Lord's vineyard. " Your fathers, where are they ? And the prophets, do they live for ever ? " Such memories are saddening. I shall do well to cease their record.

CPSIA information can be obtained
at www.ICGtesting.com
Printed in the USA
BVHW031445280219
541447BV00003B/29/P